What did my Obs

Foreword

What is more important, the training or t
personal training with your qualified Obsⅽⅰ ᵥⅽⅰ. ᵣₕᵢₛ ᵦₒₒₖₗₑₜ ᵢₛ ᵢₙₜₑₙᵈₑᵈ ₜₒ
complement the feedback an Observer will give you and help explain some of the
more advanced aspects of riding you'll be expected to demonstrate on an IAM
RoadSmart Advanced Test. It is not intended to be a comprehensive guide on how
to ride a motorcycle or prepare for the Test but it will hopefully answer some of
those questions you may not really want to ask…but the Examiner may. It also
hopefully debunks some of the myths that have grown up around the Advanced
Test (some even perpetuated by Observers) so you can concentrate on what
matters.

If you're aiming for a F1RST (awarded to those who score highly on their IAM
RoadSmart Test) then this booklet will help you prepare and offer advice on things
to practice between your Observed rides.

The contents of this booklet builds from the IAM RoadSmart Advanced Riding
Course Handbook (ARC) which you are given when you join the course. Your
Observers role, with their extended knowledge of Motorcycle Roadcraft and other
useful bits of key information, is to bring the ARC Handbook to life for you.

To get the best out of the course open your mind to concepts you may not have
tried before. The skills you develop will not only make your riding far more
enjoyable, one day they may also save your life.

Enjoy the ride!

Shaun Cronin
Regional Service Delivery Team Manager (Southern)

iAM
RoadSmart

Contents

1. Starting at the beginning

Many bikers decide that having obtained their DSA A2 or A license they want to learn more about motorcycle control and how to survive on today's busy roads. Some prefer to ride with mates to learn, perhaps wondering why they can't keep up, some read books, others seek out practical courses. The largest provider of further motorcycle coaching and testing in the UK is IAM RoadSmart. Through its local Groups this road safety charity provides coaching in line with best practise developed over many years which helps motorcyclists get more out of their machines whilst instilling skills that make them safer. Another charity that runs similar courses is the Royal Society for the Prevention of Accidents (RoSPA) and other commercial providers offer advanced riding tuition from one-day ride-outs to longer courses.

All on-the-road training must be delivered by trained instructors, many who have qualified as Police Class 1 riders themselves or in the case of the IAM RoadSmart by Institute of the Motor Industry (IMI) certified coaches, known as Observers. Usually road training takes the form of an Observer/instructor taking one or two candidates out on rides which include structured pre-ride briefs and de-briefs covering events that will have happened on the ride to highlight any learning points.

However as an student (or Associate if taking the IAM RoadSmart Advanced Riding Course) the debrief can be a bit of a blur when you come to look back on it. After all you'd done a pre-ride brief where you were told what to do and how the ride would be managed, then concentrated for a fair time whilst riding. Nerves probably also kicked-in as you're being watched and almost certainly something will have already not gone to plan that will give you and the Observer/instructor something to talk about when you stop. If the course you've chosen is a full day's riding it's going to be a pretty full-on experience and concentration levels will have to be maintained, as by the end of the day you will be pretty exhausted.

It's only natural then that by the time you get home and unfurl your run report you really can't remember the details of what was discussed on the third subject. Your Observer/instructor's notes are good but what was it that was said about planning, overtakes, white lines, pedestrian crossings?

This book assumes that in addition to any coaching you decide to undertake you will ultimately consider going for an Advanced Test, which means riding with a qualified examiner who will assess your riding skills against the standard defined to pass the Advanced Test and become a Full Member of IAM RoadSmart. It therefore describes in places what an examiner will be looking for on test - and in some places what they will not want to see. It's structured in a question and answer format to help address those questions you may have but perhaps don't want to ask.

2. The Basics

There are a few basics which your Observer will cover with you during your first few rides. One that often crops up is how you sit on your bike. Quite a few riders are unaware that they don't sit on their bike properly, something that is quickly obvious from behind. It could be because a rider is compensating for an old injury so they sit off-centre or a common mistake is to place their feet with the instep of their boots the foot pegs with their toes pointing downwards - Donald Duck like. Another, seen particularly on sports bikes, is riding with straight arms, elbows locked, restricting the ability to control the bike and increasing the effort required to turn the handlebars.

Your Observer will ensure that these things are all discussed and addressed and then you're ready for the off. But what about when you come to a stop?

When I stop which foot should I put down?

The 'Safety Position' (that is with the left leg down and the right foot on the rear brake) has been taught by generations of CSM trained CBT/DAS instructors whose approach is that anything other than left foot down is 100% wrong.

However, many IAM Observers advise putting the right foot down to make selecting neutral and then a gear to pull away much easier.

Then there's the 'Hendon Shuffle' which came out of the Hendon Police school and involves a right foot down, left foot up, to get out of gear at a standstill, then left foot down, right foot up to cover brake. Then the same procedure to get back into gear to pull away. The theory is that you are covering a brake all the time you are stationary. Alternatively you could use the front brake.

So what does the IAM Examiner want to see?

It has never been a requirement of the test to do a 'Hendon Shuffle'. When coming to a stop it is immaterial which foot is placed on the ground first or leaves it last providing the machine is stopped safely, smoothly and in control and is moved away from rest in a similar fashion.

The pros and cons of each, which may affect your choice depending on circumstances, are:

Left leg down first:

+ hill starts are much easier using the back brake, so maybe choose if stopping on an incline

+ allows the use of the rear brake for improved stability and slow speed control, for instance when filtering in traffic or at walking pace where you might have to stop and start regularly, or when descending a steep hill

+ allows you to show a brake light, improving visibility to traffic behind

+ holding the bike on the rear brake possibly reduces the risk of losing control if you are hit at low speed from behind

− you have to do the 'Hendon Shuffle' to get out of gear and back in to gear - rather tedious and often unnecessary, and in certain circumstances where you may need to move of smartly (eg if you have filtered to the front of a queue) potentially dangerous.

Right leg down first:

+ you can get in and out of gear easily

+ you can gently hold the front brake for the visibility effect of the brake light

+ you should hold the front brake on so a tap from behind will not send the bike shooting out from underneath you as you WILL put your foot down to recover balance if using the rear brake

- you can't use the back brake so have to rely on the front brake only when coming to a halt, so you have to be effective at feathering the brake to avoid the front forks diving

- hill starts are much more difficult using the front brake.

Should I always select neutral when stopped?

Not necessarily. Neutral should be selected when you are likely to be stationary for some time. This counts towards the test competencies of Vehicle Sympathy that the Examiner will be looking at. To not select neutral will not attract adverse marking on its own but might contribute with other faults to an adverse test result overall.

So best practise is to select neutral if you are going to be stopped for some time, ie. the traffic lights have just changed to red in front of you, or a line of school children have started using a pedestrian crossing ahead.

Do I need to put a foot down at STOP lines?

There actually isn't a specific requirement to place a foot on the ground at a STOP line, however the essential requirement is that your bike has come to a complete STOP. Planners only put STOP lines where they have determined there is a serious risk of a conflict. The purpose is to enable you to gather the information safely and correctly before proceeding. Only you can judge if you can maintain stability and control of the bike when at a complete standstill without placing a foot on the ground.

3. White Lines and the Highway Code

This is one of the most popular areas with examiners when asking the Highway Code questions at test - when can you, and when can't you, cross white lines. It can start with the simple question; *"What is the difference between a Centre line and a Hazard line?"* Immediately the brain starts whizzing around; *"What the hell is a Hazard line? My Observer never told me about those."*

The Highway Code defines a Centre line as a broken white line which marks the centre of the road. When this becomes longer and the gaps shorten it means there is a hazard ahead. It happens before bends, junctions, etc. So basically, if there is more white paint than gap it's a Hazard line. If there's more gap than paint it's a Centre line.

Then the examiner may ask the follow-on question; *"Can you overtake on a Hazard line?"* As the hazard line doesn't indicate to which hazard it applies, you the rider must determine this. Generally the more paint and signs around the more dangerous the hazard. However if you're on a country road and have just passed the junction to which they refer, and it's safe to do so, yes you can overtake on a Hazard line as they extend both sides of the junction. Clearly to overtake before the junction on the Hazard line is probably not such a wise move.

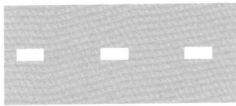

Centre Line

Hazard Line

Single Solid Line

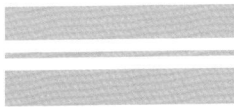

Double Solid Line

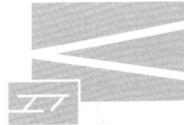

Hatched Areas

Solid White Lines

Then the examiner, warming to his subject, may ask; *"When may you cross a solid white line?"* Ah you think, time for the get-out-of-jail-free card; *"When instructed to do so by a traffic or police officer"* you confidently reply. *"And the other cases where you may?"* he asks' …. hmmm….

You may cross a solid white line when it is safe to do so and will not bring you into conflict with other traffic on three occasions:

- Turning right into a driveway or junction, but you must not straddle the white line whilst waiting;

9

- To pass a stationary vehicle(s) - **Note queuing traffic is not considered to fall into this category, so no filtering over a solid white line**; and finally;

- To pass a bicycle, horse or road maintenance vehicle not travelling at more than 10mph.

You may overtake moving traffic (or filter) by staying on your side of a solid white line provided there is sufficient space between the vehicle being overtaken and the white line and provided it is done safely and you do not come into conflict or cause confusion with other road users.

Crossing a solid white line under any other circumstances, such as at the end of an overtake will result in a test failure - so don't do it!

Hatched Areas

Areas of diagonal white lines, or chevrons are there to separate traffic lanes and to protect traffic turning right. If the area is bordered by a broken white line you should not enter the area unless it is necessary and it is safe to do so. You could argue that it was both safe and necessary to enter such an area to perform an overtake. However, the argument of necessity may be challenged should a conflict result and it could be determined that you contributed to the outcome by your actions so make doubly sure it's safe before entering these areas.

Clearly if the area is surrounded by a solid white line you must not enter the area except in an emergency.

Cycle Lanes

Be aware if a solid white lines defines the edge of a cycle lane. The highway code says you MUST NOT ride or stop in a cycle lane marked by a solid white line during

You mustn't ride or stop in cycle lanes defined by a solid white line

Remember to stop at the first STOP line - You're not a bicycle

its times of operation. Also do not ride or stop in a cycle lane marked by a broken white line unless it is unavoidable.

Finally, at traffic lights ensure you stop at the first stop line if a box is marked out for cyclists beyond it. Motorcycles are not bicycles and you will fail your test if you stop within this reserved area.

4. The Limit Point and moving to get the 'view'

The Limit Point is the furthest point you can see on the road across unbroken tarmac. This governs your speed as at all times you should be able to stop within that distance, on your side of the road. There are exceptions, for example on single track roads where this distance is halved. So naturally if you can position your bike on the road to extend the Limit Point you can go faster - Yes?

In manoeuvring to extend your view and the limit point though, where can you move across the centre line of the road? What is 'off-siding' and 'straight-lining' and when can you use these techniques?

Off-siding

Firstly, 'off-siding' is when you purposely move across the centre line/hazard line, (or in the absence of such a line, the centre of the carriageway) in order to extend your view.

Where's the Limit Point here?

On single track roads, where there is no possibility of passing an oncoming vehicle due to the width of the road, it is acceptable to cross the centre line of the road, providing it is both advantageous and gives no risk of conflict in order to enable you to be seen earlier by other road users and for you to see on-coming traffic.

However, on two-way carriageways (normal A and B roads) experience is showing that moving across the centre line of the road when, for example approaching a left-hand bend at the end of a straight, is causing riders to put themselves in danger.

Where as this was a technique taught many years ago by some Police Training Schools, IAM RoadSmart now actively discourages this practice and it is therefore not acceptable on test to move right of the centre line for a left-hand bend.

The exception would be if having performed an overtake you were already over the centre line and hence have a view around the approaching bend. In this situation you may stay in an off-side position rather than move back to the near-side of the road which would shorten your view. So if you have the view due to your position you may keep it but you can't purposely move over the centre line in order to gain the view.

Bends - Straight-lining/Trimming

'Trimming' or 'Straight-lining' a set of open bends is an effective way of making progress whilst keeping the bike upright in a stable position with minimal input. It also helps preserve an extended view through the bends to the limit point. However, the rider must be constantly aware of any areas of potential 'dead-ground' within the bends where your view is restricted and where vulnerable road users may be (horses, cyclists, pedestrians, etc) or other hazards. Your view should always be from kerb-to-kerb throughout if straight-lining a set of bends.

Straight-lining must not be carried out if there is a risk of conflict with other road users or where it will inconvenience, confuse, or cause alarm or distress, to others.

If you compromise your own or any other road user's safety you will fail the test.

Roundabouts – Straight- lining/trimming

'Trimming' or 'Straight- lining' roundabouts is often encouraged to enhance safety, stability and progress on a motorcycle. This is correct if the situation is appropriate, for example on mini-roundabouts, in the wet or where fuel spillages may have occurred.

This must not however be carried out if it will inconvenience, confuse or where there is a risk of conflict with other road users. The risk from traffic approaching from the rear is also a serious consideration in the decision as to whether to 'straighten' a roundabout especially if moving outside of the defined lane you are currently occupying.

You should avoid touching or riding over the white paint used in the centre of mini-roundabouts. Motorcycles are deemed to be manoeuvrable enough to travel around roundabouts, not over them, or worse still if turning right, cutting across and going the 'wrong-way' around them.

You should always aim to remain in the safest position on the road. If a vehicle is waiting to enter the roundabout from another road and the safest route means you cross the white paint the examiner would consider if this was the safest option. If after a de-briefing you had convinced him this was done for the right reasons, he could still pass you. If though you ride over a roundabout for no reason other than convenience the examiner will fail you.

As always, if you compromise your own, or any other road user's safety, the examiner will fail you.

5. Speed Limits

Speed limits – simple, aren't they? The authorities put up big round signs by the roadside and every bike manufacturer fits a device on the handlebars that tells you how fast you're going. If you keep the needle or number displayed at or below the figure in the big round sign you remain legal. Except you're riding a machine that has the power to weight ratio of a supercar and can probably break all legal road speed limits in second gear…. So the challenge becomes one of restraint, and skill, learning where you can use the agility that gives you and showing you can tame all that performance.

Speed Limits

Years ago, in a galaxy far, far, away, when many long-time Observers took their tests, examiners were possibly more flexible about speed. It was often heard that the examiner would 'not be looking at their speedometer during overtakes' and as Associates we were advised to clarify what the examiner was happy with speed wise during the pre-ride brief.

Well, that has all changed. Now at no point during your test must you exceed the legal speed limit or you will fail. During the briefing, an examiner will probably use the phrase 'Safe, Systematic, Smooth and Legal'. The clue is in the final word - legal. So it's important you know at all times what the speed limit is for the road you're riding on, and if not, what clues you can quickly use to determine what it could be.

Often there are signs each side of the road but one still makes it legal

SatNavs are allowed on test but you shouldn't rely on them to indicate the in-force speed limit as they're often incorrect and you will probably be on roads you are not familiar with, so get used to reading the road signs to know the limit, rather than that nice little screen on your handlebars. You may want to practice switching off your SatNav during rides leading up to your test so you get used to doing this.

Beware also that speed limit changes often take place at 'T' junctions. So as well as performing a turn you should be looking for those big round signs which tell you the limit in force for the road you are joining.

Slowing for a lower speed limit

- Should you use your brakes to reduce speed into a lower limit?
- Should a brake light be shown when slowing for hazards or a change in speed limits?

Well, it depends on how much speed you need to lose over what distance, and if there's following traffic.

'Acceleration Sense' should be used where practical as part of a smooth, yet progressive ride. In many urban situations when slowing from say a 40mph to a 30mph limit, there may be no need to brake if the manoeuvre has been planned properly, unless it is considered necessary for a brake light to be shown to traffic following too closely or approaching too fast.

However when slowing from a National to a 30mph limit, simply rolling off the throttle to slow may mean starting the process some way-off the actual limit change, affecting progress, so a smooth application of the brakes should be used when necessary. Remember it's 'brakes to slow' and 'gears to go', so no changing down through the gearbox to obtain engine braking just to avoid using the brakes. Manufacturers provide brakes for a reason. They're cheaper to replace than gearboxes and engines and they are more effective. What's more the examiner will expect you to show you know how to use them.

Where does the limit start?

The point at which a speed limit starts or ends is at the change of limit signs. When entering a lower limit the correct speed should have been achieved when you pass between the signs. Any braking should have been completed and to continue to show a brake light after the limit change indicates your speed was too high when passing the limit signs, a simple giveaway to the examiner. Any necessary gear changes should be undertaken after, or at the end of the braking phase, as per IPSGA. (Your Observer will have told you about IPSGA).

Where a speed limit sign is obscured, or can only be seen very late, the examiner will expect you to slow to the limit promptly and will make allowances for the situation accordingly. However, a failure for you to see limits signs early enough if visible will be considered poor observation.

Accelerating to a higher limit

This should be the easy bit - right? When increasing speed to a higher limit, judging how fast to accelerate can be difficult.

Should it be 'race-like', or more sedate as I'm being examined?

Well, this is Advanced Riding so taking a mile or so to get to the National limit from a 40mph zone on a clear road is not really demonstrating confidence or great self-awareness. Acceleration should be brisk rather than fast but also be smooth, progressive and controlled with regard to the prevailing conditions.

Acceleration should only start when you've passed the limits signs indicating a higher limit, not 20 metres beforehand, nor should there be a slow drift upwards over the last 100 metres towards the signs.

What is the correct speed?

It is thought by some that you must demonstrate good progress at all times and therefore you need to compensate for any over-reading of your bike's speedometer, so riding with an indicated speed 10% above the actual speed limit is a good thing. This is wrong.

As described in the Advanced Rider Course handbook section 'What to Expect on Test' you should at all times rely on your speedometer and not make any adjustments for perceived inaccuracy - even if you have a SatNav with speed indication. The Examiner will realise if your speedometer reads differently to his own and will make allowances, unless it's a significant defect which would make the bike unroadworthy.

Remember that the speed limit is a maximum not a target speed. If road conditions require it, slow down and only return to the limit speed when safe to do so.

You may be marked down for not making sufficient progress (which requires a significant wider set of skills than just speed) but you will definitely be failed for exceeding a speed limit.

What speed should I do when overtaking?

Overtaking is covered in the next two chapters, but regarding speed, you should not embark on an overtake with the intention of breaking the speed limit. Of course if things change once you've started the manoeuvre, you must take the safest course of action, which may mean accelerating hard to get past. However, expect the examiner to question your observation and planning when you de-brief at the end.

Finally, when overtaking there's no limit on the speed differential between you and the target vehicle. Overtaking should be carried out briskly and safely as conditions allow whilst remaining within the applicable speed limit. This means being in the right gear and the right place at the right time. Now, where have you heard that before?

6. Filtering

Overtaking and filtering, when to, when not to, and how to do it well are complex subjects and all depend on the actual situation you find yourself in. No one else can see exactly what you can see or knows your own and your bike's abilities better than yourself. As with all the advice in this booklet, these chapters on overtaking should be read in conjunction with the relevant chapters in the IAM RoadSmart Advanced Rider Course handbook and discussed with your Observer.

Overtaking and filtering are probably the most variable aspects of the advanced test. The examiner can't manufacture an overtaking opportunity, nor arrange for traffic to be queuing conveniently at a set of lights during the test. Therefore it's not necessary to perform either an overtake or filtering on your test. However, the advanced rider should be able to demonstrate good forward observation and planning by actively looking for opportunities and showing the examiner that they are by bike position and rider actions. Of course, if clear filtering and/or overtake situations arise, the advanced rider is expected to skilfully execute them, helping to demonstrate progress.

Filtering

Up ahead you see the traffic lights have just turned red. It's a busy dual carriageway with two lanes on each side and you're in a convoy of vehicles nose-to-tail. To control the speed of the traffic arriving at the lights you move smoothly to the outside lane and slow slightly to give yourself time and space to assess the situation developing. The traffic ahead comes to a stop leaving a nice filtering opportunity down between the two lanes. You smoothly, and without excess speed, filter between the two lanes to the front of the queue, arriving just as the lights turn green. Without putting a foot down, you accelerate away, checking to the left and right for any late crossing traffic. It feels nice and a smile breaks out under the visor.

You assessed the opportunity early, controlled yours and others entry speed into the developing situation, picked a landing spot before starting filtering, which was at the front of the queue, and smoothly executed the manoeuvre. Had the lights turned green before you reached the front, you had already decided to smoothly re-join the traffic as gaps opened between the cars as they pulled away.

If the gap between the traffic had been too narrow to filter on your GS with panniers, you'd have demonstrated to the examiner that you were looking down the middle by moving your bike and your head to indicate you were looking, and then smoothly pulling up behind the rear-most vehicle. Now examiners are only normal people and don't have mind-reading abilities. If you'd just pulled up in-line at the rear of the queue you'd have demonstrated nothing about your planning. The examiner may think you didn't even consider filtering. Don't ham it up, but it's probably a good thing to give some clues to the chap following you about what's going on inside your head as you ride the test.

Further on another queue develops outside a school. It's pick-up time and cars are stopping in front of you. There's no on-coming traffic so you go for it, pulling out into the opposite lane and you start filtering. Without warning a car pulls out from the school entrance between two cars and comes towards you. There's no gap to escape into and you're left stranded in the opposite lane. It's all very embarrassing as you try to miss the mirror of the nearside car as the on-coming driver waves her appreciation accompanied with a death stare and words the ear plugs save you from.

On checking your mirrors the examiner is nowhere to be seen as he waits way back behind the queue. Not such a good feeling this time. So a combination of poor observation, planning, and not having a landing spot identified before you set off or a plan B all combine to make this a moment you would prefer to forget.

If you think filtering may be on, look ahead, plan the manoeuvre, including having a landing spot and an alternative escape plan if things change before you get there. Don't assume other road users have seen you. If it's not on, you've hopefully demonstrated to the examiner by your position that you've looked and decided not to go.

What's the difference between filtering and making progress at speed between traffic?

Filtering is passing vehicles that are stationary or moving below a speed of 20mph with a difference in speed of 10 to 15mph. It is legal. If a bike travels between lanes of traffic moving at higher speeds (as you might have seen others do commuting on motorways) with a high speed differential between it and the other traffic, possibly also weaving from lane to lane, the Police may look at it as Riding without Due Care and Attention - Section 3 of the Road Traffic Act. If really dangerous, it would be obvious to a competent and careful rider, and the Police could consider it Dangerous Riding. So it is illegal and dangerous, as the bike appears quickly to other road users and may be unsighted to a driver who can change lane quickly due to the speed their vehicle is travelling at, and the rider could be disqualified or even imprisoned - serious stuff indeed.

Can I filter to the front of a queue waiting at a pedestrian crossing?

The Highway Code says you may filter up to the rear of the vehicle immediately adjacent to the stop line (the front-most vehicle) and no further. You must then follow that vehicle across the crossing. So you can't filter to the front of the queue but you can filter on the zig-zag lines up to the rear of the front-most vehicle if there is a landing spot for you to safely enter on your side of the centre line. In these areas don't be tempted to filter past slow moving vehicles within the zig-zag lines as this could be viewed as overtaking, which is not legal in these areas.

At pedestrian crossings do not pass the front-most vehicle.

7. Overtaking

The thing about overtaking is you can't do it by making a decision and starting to accelerate from a following position of 2 seconds behind the target vehicle. By the time you've changed into the right gear and accelerated the opportunity will probably have gone and the speed differential could be too great for you to smoothly abandon the manoeuvre. Bikes are agile things but you have to plan the overtake as shown in the Advanced Rider Course (ARC) handbook to make that agility work for you, and for more overtakes to become possible.

Overtaking is a demonstration of skill, not speed or power. Planning ahead and being in the right position at the right time will mean you can achieve smooth legal overtakes without a negative perception by other road users.

Having seen the right-hand bend ahead and looking over the hedge to the right, you see a straight section of road after the bend. As the vehicle ahead slows for the bend you move up to the overtake position (1 second behind). You change down a gear, and keep to the left of the bend to extend your view and to avoid being directly behind the target vehicle. As the bend opens up, the road is clear and you drop out from behind the vehicle to Position 3 and being in the right gear then accelerate smoothly past. The move took less than 100m on the road and you were back on your side of the road well before you were even 1/3rd of the way down the straight. If you'd waited for the straight to open up to see there was no on-coming traffic and only then moved up to the overtake position (1 second behind) the opportunity would have been lost as the next bend approached.

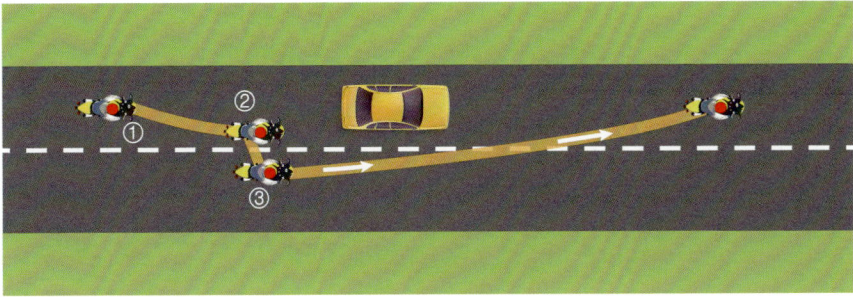

The 3 Position Overtake

Overtaking is one of those skills that can only be perfected by practise. Hunting down subject vehicles can be fun, and executing a clean overtake that ticks all the SLAP boxes is satisfying. SLAP you ask? Was it Safe? Was it Legal? Did you gain some Advantage? What was the Perception of other road users to your manoeuvre?

This is when it tends to go wrong for riders who are keen to demonstrate an overtake on test. When approaching a slower vehicle riders tend to go direct to the overtaking position (2), even if there is no immediate likelihood of an overtake. Initially you should take up the appropriate following position (1) and from there, when the situation is appropriate, and if required, make a decision to move into the overtaking position.

The following and overtaking position can be one and the same if circumstances require, such as when following a larger vehicle which you can't see over, around or through. If you closed up to the overtaking position (2) your view would become restricted. If you had a greater following distance then you have a better view and be able to execute the overtake sooner.

When I get to 'Position 3' what am I looking for before deciding to go?

- There's no on-coming traffic
- You have kerb-to-kerb view and they are unbroken on either side, which could indicate there's a drive or junction from which a vehicle could emerge
- There's not a speed limit change or zebra crossing ahead which will require you to brake harshly
- The next bend is far enough away for you to slow if necessary without adversely affecting the target vehicle
- There's no dead ground ahead which could hide another road user (horses, pedestrians, cyclists etc) who has been masked by the target vehicle and could cause it to pull out.

23

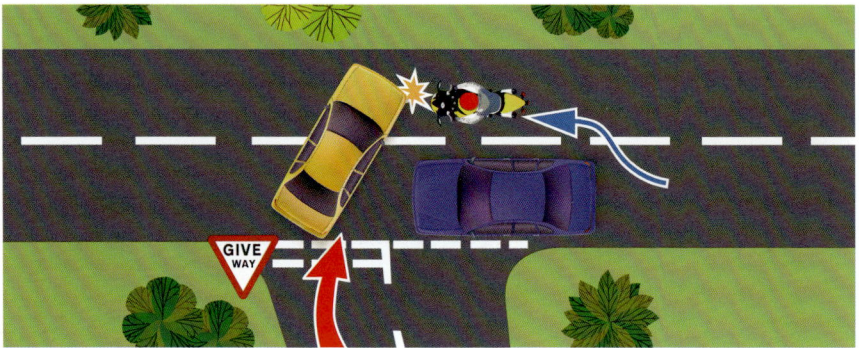

Do not overtake when approaching junctions

That sounds like quite a few things, but with experience it only takes a second or so as you match the target vehicles speed and avoids those embarrassing harsh braking moments as you try to pull back in behind.

The Momentum Overtake

A momentum overtake is when there are no hazards and you are able to approach and overtake the subject vehicle in one smooth manoeuvre. The 3-stage overtake is used when the situation does not allow a momentum overtake making it necessary to match the speed and follow the subject vehicle in front while you plan your overtake.

But when is it appropriate to use a momentum overtake, and what are the advantages?

If you assess a momentum overtake is going to be possible, adopt a position that gives you the best view and opportunity to overtake. Consider your speed of approach. Is it appropriate? Make sure you're in a gear that makes the bike responsive enough for the overtake. Finally, apply an appropriate degree of acceleration to overtake safely and return to your side of the road.

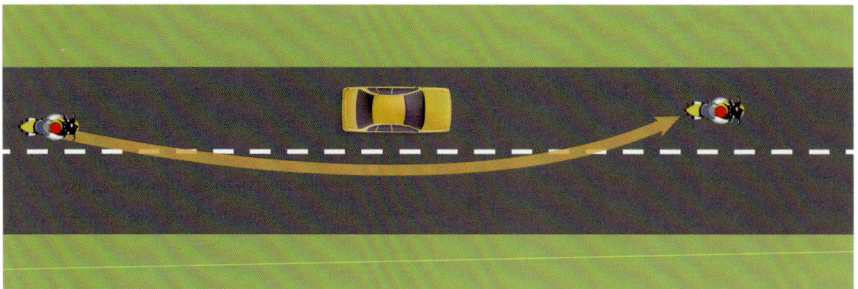

The Momentum Overtake

So there you have it. If you assess an overtake is immediately possible and you can approach and complete the manoeuvre smoothly, use a momentum overtake. If you're unsure, unsighted or have to match and follow the subject vehicle the 3-stage should be used. However, consider at what following distance you get the best view yet are close enough to execute the overtake when an opportunity arises. Don't close up on the subject vehicle when there's no chance of an overtake and don't fall into the trap of swooping into the pass by accelerating towards the subject vehicle. The examiner will not be impressed and you will fail your test.

Should I use my indicators when overtaking?

Indicators need only be used when they would be of benefit to other road users. Would the driver of the vehicle in front have even seen your indicator? Wouldn't a big bright headlight in their mirror have alerted them to your presence and if not, would a little winking indicator have made any difference?

Also consider if using your indicator early would confuse oncoming traffic; 'Has that bike seen me or is he going to attempt to go between me and the car he's following?'

So generally there's no need to use your indicators when overtaking unless it will help someone else, maybe another bike following you for example.

When overtaking how fast can I go?

For advice on the maximum speed when overtaking and the speed differential between you and the vehicle you're overtaking, read Chapter 4 on speed limits.

8. Motorways

Are motorways different?

Motorways probably represent a unique riding environment. Some aspects are a positive, like the ability to cover large distances relatively quickly, but they also pose additional challenges to the motorcyclist.

Greater distances between rest and refuelling stops; high noise levels due to the speed you're travelling at and from adjacent vehicles also travelling at speed; the dangers of stopping on the hard shoulder should you have a mechanical failure; possible high volumes of traffic coupled with the challenges of filtering if traffic comes to a halt; high levels of spray and reduced vision if the roads are wet; and generally the absence of bends to add interest to the ride.

This means many riders choose routes which avoid motorways but all of us will at sometime ride on them. That could be regularly commuting into London or just occasionally getting back home from a ride-out with friends.

Motorway riding can be divided into three phases; joining, behaviour whilst on them, and the leaving process.

Joining

When the on-ramp has two lanes the advice generally is to use the lane that gives you the best view of the road you're joining. This means if the on-ramp comes from above the motorway use the outside lane so you can look down onto the motorway to judge your entry point and speed to join the traffic smoothly without causing any disruption. However be aware of any vehicles on your near-side and ensure you don't block their access onto the motorway.

If the on-ramp comes from below consider using the left-hand lane so once you've reached the level of the main carriageway you have the maximum time and space to plan how you join the traffic. Of course you need to watch out for vehicles in the right-hand lane which may block your access so good

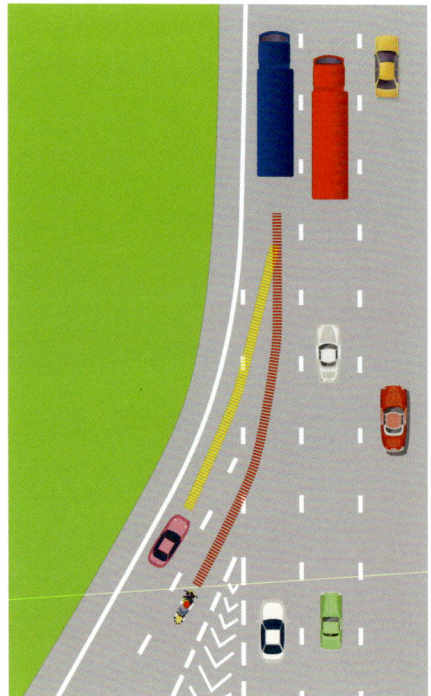

observation, situational awareness and planning is called for.

Once on the motorway

Once you're on the motorway you will be travelling at high speed and so you need to stay alert and maintain good all-round observation, especially as far forwards as possible. Maintain your safety bubble and observe the two second rule when following vehicles. Give clear indications if changing lane, and if moving out from lane 1 into lane 2 be aware of vehicles moving back from lane 3 to lane 2 which you may come into conflict with.

Travelling at 70mph, as you will be on test, you will probably not be the fastest moving vehicle but you will be overtaking HGVs and other vehicles in lane 1.

How frequently do you move back into the lane to your left?

The guidance is to avoid constantly changing lane and to remain in your current lane if moving left would mean you travelling for less than 10 seconds before having to pull out again. Now 10 seconds at 70mph is actually quite a long time - try counting it the next time you're on a motorway.

Remain aware of weather conditions which can change particularly if you're on a long journey. Wind effects around tall HGVs can cause your bike to move around, particularly in high side-winds or over viaducts and tall bridges. A setting sun can also present difficulties especially if the road is wet reflecting bright light into your eyes. In most cases the answer is to slow down and take greater care.

Remember that long journeys on motorways on a motorbike can be tiring and your concentration can begin to drop. Take regular breaks to rehydrate, eat and to check your bike over.

Leaving at your junction

Leaving a motorway requires planning, starting probably before you even left home or the last stop.

Which junction are you planning to leave at?

Are you looking for a junction number, a road number, or town/city name?

On long journeys are you able to countdown to the junction you plan to take? Junction signs generally appear 1 mile and 1/2 mile before the off-ramp. At the 1 mile sign before your junction begin planning the process to leave the motorway.

Where in the traffic are you going to move into lane 1? Can you get past that HGV and caravan?

Generally I advise Associates to be in lane 1 at the 1/2 mile sign so they are able to start signalling to leave the motorway at the 300m board. If this means following a slower vehicle than so be it but you must avoid sweeping across multiple lanes and traffic to access the off-ramp at the last moment.

Once on the off-ramp, generally not before, you can start slowing for the inevitable junction that will appear.

A common question asked by examiners at test is 'What colours are the reflectors between the different parts of a motorway?

- **Red** between Lane 1 and the hard shoulder.

- **Green** between Lane 1 and exit and entry lanes

- **White** between running lanes 1 - 3

- **Orange** between the outermost lane and the central reservation.

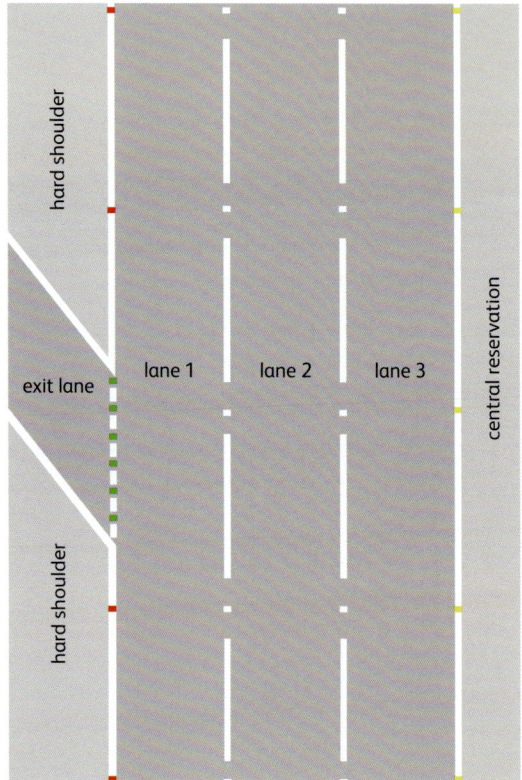

9. Brrrr.....Winter Riding

Winter riding and the varying conditions dictate some different thinking when out on the road with regards to your riding, your kit and the weather.

As the nights draw in and the temperature begins to drop, many riders call it a day and pack up their bike and gear for the winter. However, I often hear statements like 'There's no such thing as bad weather, just inappropriate clothing' and, 'As advanced riders we do it all year round,' both of which are true in parts. But as an advanced rider out and about during the coming months, what additional aspects of riding should you be aware of?

Appropriate clothing

In summer the airflow jacket and summer gloves were a godsend, but already these are at the back of the cupboard and the textiles are back on, which is great until the first really cold morning when an early start is required for a long ride ahead. Cold weather is dangerous. As your body's core cools, your thinking becomes slower and reaction times get longer. The body starts to protect the vital organs so blood circulation to the extremities like your hands and feet reduce, and they lose most of their sensitivity. The result is you lose control of them. Hypothermia alone can kill, riding a motorcycle while hypothermic is not big or clever, so always be self-aware and recognise if you're getting cold, and take action.

Wear multiple insulating thin layers, but ensure you retain enough movement for effective control and observation. Avoid clothes that make you sweat, as damp clothing under a waterproof layer can make you even colder. Outdoor stores sell a range of base and intermediate layer garments which work just as well on the bike and are cheaper than some of the fancy motorbike brands.

Ensure you close all the zips and fasteners to prevent ballooning, including pockets. Keep your head, hands and feet well insulated. If you regularly travel distances in winter, consider the use of electrically heated gloves or the jackets. Remember if you feel you are getting cold find somewhere sheltered to stop, warm up and maybe have a hot drink.

Weather

Collisions are often blamed on bad weather, but the real cause is human error. You must ride according to the conditions and deal with these safely. This starts before you start out. Check the forecast, anticipate changes that may occur during your journey, and if necessary check the weather again during your journey. There are many free weather apps you can download to do this including *RainToday* which gives real-time rainfall maps for the whole of the UK.

The weather affects both you and your machine. How far can you see, how fast are your reactions and what level of grip do your tyres have?

Riding in Poor Visibility

Do you commute? Is the low sun always in your eyes when riding east in the morning or west in the evening? If it's a social ride, could you plan a west in the morning and east in the afternoon route during these shorter days to avoid this? Other examples of weather that reduces visibility are fog, mist, heavy rain, road spray, falling snow and sleet. When weather reduces your visibility, reduce your speed so you can still stop within the distance you can see to be clear on your side of the road. Regularly check your actual speed on the speedometer, as it can drift upwards without the usual reference points. Ensure your headlight and rear lights are all working and are clean and bright. Keep good rearward observation for vehicles that want to travel using your rear light to navigate with, or worse, are approaching from behind at speed as they may not have seen you.

Focus on the edge of the carriageway, hazard lines, and cat's eyes to help guide where the road goes, especially near junctions or corners. Staring into a featureless mist, you will quickly lose any sense of where you are and your eyes will get tired. Focus on what you can see, but avoid being drawn into just looking at the lights of the vehicle in front. The distance between you could quickly reduce and you could collide with it if it stops suddenly.

Fog, mist, cold weather and rain can all cause your visor to mist up on the inside. This further reduces your visibility. Riding with your visor up is not practical in cold weather as your eyes begin to stream with water and you can get cold very quickly. Use anti-misting spray on both surfaces of the visor. Pin-lock double glazed visors significantly reduce misting, but if it still occurs raise your visor a fraction to increase the airflow over the inner surface. You can also try fitting a nose-guard to your helmet to direct your warm, damp breath downwards. Clearly, riding with a tinted or smoked visor at night or in poor visibility is just stupid!

Road Surfaces

Weather and road surface combine to affect the level of tyre grip your bike will have, and could also affect the handling. We've all experienced a wet road and expect a reduction of some kind in the grip available. This changes depending on the road surface type and in winter a further reduction in grip will occur due to colder tyre temperatures. If salt has been spread to disperse ice, the resulting wet road will have a further reduction in grip due to the emulsion that water and salt form when mixed. If you don't believe me, try using an eye wash without salt in the water. It's the salt in your tears that enable your eyelids to glide painlessly open and shut! The same will happen to your tyres if you don't allow for it.

Always look well ahead to identify changes in road surface, and adapt accordingly. Control of your bike depends on tyre grip for steering, braking, acceleration and banking. Adjust the demands you make on your tyres grip according to the changing conditions. If your bike has different mode settings, read and understand the effects they have on handling. Selecting rain mode may not only flatten the engine's torque delivery but could adjust the ABS and traction control settings to be more sensitive.

Common road surfaces that can cause a hazard for motorcyclists are tar-banding around road repairs, mud, wet leaves, drain covers, diesel spills - especially on roundabouts - smooth shiny areas (especially when wet) where the tar 'puddled' during the recent hot summer, and road-marking paint. Look out for pot-holes or puddles of water which may conceal one. Hitting a pot-hole at any speed can damage a wheel and be seriously dangerous for the rider.

If you fail to spot one of these and can't avoid them, slow down on the approach if possible and pass over them with care, trying not to put steering, braking, or acceleration inputs into the bike while you cross them. Harsh steering or braking can destabilise the bike, especially if the grip is

already compromised.

Weather conditions can cause ice to form on the road. Ice comes in many forms, but generally you can't see black ice, while white haw-frost you can. Look out for both types under trees and in other shaded areas even when the sun has been out for some time and melted it everywhere else. Generally bikes and snow or ice don't mix...

Night Rider

Strangely it's harder to see in the dark than in daylight. Observation therefore requires a different level of skill to be effective. Contrast levels fall and edges become less distinct. Motorcycles generally have poor headlights, so your visibility is reduced in range. It's no longer possible to pick out hedge lines way up ahead or the camber of the road so clearly. Night riding also puts additional strain on your eyes and highlights any defects in focus you may have. Ensure you've had your eyes tested recently. Being able to read a number plate at 20 metres in sunlight may not be good enough to ride a country road safely at night.

Ensure you have a clear visor and it's clean and unscratched. Same for all your lights. Are they clean, working, bright and correctly adjusted? Use main beam on unlit roads but remember to dip it for other road users, including when following another vehicle. You may also find a dipped headlight more effective if riding in mist, fog, snow or sleet, as it reduces the reflected glare.

Think about your clothing. Hi-vis generally doesn't work at night as it appears black or grey under artificial light. What you need is reflective clothing.

Does your riding gear have good reflective areas?

Are these clean and visible?

Rucksacks generally mask any reflective areas on jackets, so if you use one be aware and consider fitting a top box with reflective tape if riding regularly at night and need to carry 'stuff'.

Overall

As the more challenging conditions of winter approach, think about if your journey is really necessary on the bike if poor weather is forecast. If necessary take the bus, car, train, or even walk. Examiners will cancel tests if the forecast is to be below 5c on the day. There's a reason for this, as there are old riders and bold riders, but no old, bold riders. And examiners are generally the former.

However, winter riding on those lovely bright, clear days can be fun. It presents new challenges for the thinking rider which with care and consideration you can master and reap the rewards. Prepare well, enjoy the ride, and a hot coffee generally tastes better at the end.

10. Are You Fit to Ride?

So when do motorcycle riders have to take an MOT? Well never. Unless you reach a certain age or have a declared medical condition you probably have never had someone check out your suitability to go riding. Providing your license permits it you can merrily throw a leg over a 190bhp bike with performance most supercars can only dream of and ride off into the sunrise.

But are you safe? Who's responsible for checking you out? After all we know who's responsible for checking the bike is safe - POWDDERSS is driven home by all our Observers so your bike should have brakes that work, tyres that are legal, a chain that is well adjusted and lights that work. The only check you might have had done by an Observer on yourself was the eyesight test. Can you read a number plate at 20 metres? We don't even ask can you see two of them, just the letters and numbers and the order they come in.

Dive to the back of Motorcycle RoadCraft though and there is a comprehensive check list for us, the riders. I AM SAFE covers it but how many of us pat ourselves down before firing up the motor, especially if it was a long night last night and you're riding with friends who plan to leave just after breakfast?

Ask yourself these questions:

I - Illness   Do I have an illness or symptoms that might affect my ability to ride?

A - Attitude   How do I feel about this journey? Am I fully focussed on the riding? Are there human factors or distractions I need to take into account?

M - Medication   Am I taking any medication that might affect my riding? Hay fever tablets etc.

S - Sleep   Was last night a long one? Am I suffering from fatigue or lack of sleep?

A - Alcohol   Did I drink a lot last night? Am I still affected by alcohol?

F - Food   Am I hungry or thirsty? Could low blood sugar or dehydration affect my judgement?

E - Emotion   Am I angry, depressed or stressed? Could this lead me to take risks?

There are many versions of these self checklists. Use the one that works for you but importantly act on the information you gain. If you are a bit hung-over and tired after a long ride yesterday face up to it and make the right decision. No-one will mind if you opt to sit out a morning's ride to have a late breakfast if it means everyone is safe. You can always join a ride later in the day.

Better still of course is to think ahead and plan, just like when on the bike. Pack yourself off to bed early the night before to get a few zzzzzs in so you're bright eyed and bushy-tailed the next morning.

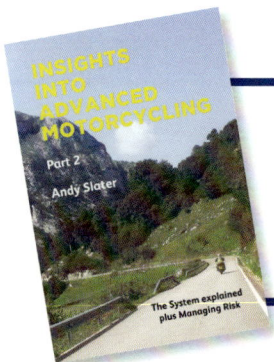

**Insights into Advanced Motorcycling
Part 2
is now available from
eBay, Amazon, and many IAM Groups**

11. The Thinking Rider

If you dig into the back of a copy of *Motorcycle Roadcraft*, on which all Advanced Riding is based, you will find a matrix outlining the Goals for Driver Education. This is a framework which sets out the competences that driver/rider training should focus on to produce the safest riders possible.

It separates riding into four levels of competence. The first is controlling your machine. Can you operate the controls smoothly, do you sit on the bike correctly, can you control your progress and stop? Secondly, can you control your bike in the wider traffic environment; observing, planning, signalling, obeying the rules of the road and positioning to make progress? Mastering these two competencies are central to passing the IAM RoadSmart Advanced test.

The Driver Education Matrix and IAM RoadSmart Advanced Riding Course (ARC) both identify a third competence called Human Factors. This looks at possibly the most valuable component on the bike - you !

- *What attitudes do you have to riding, the law and other road users?*

- *Are you aware of how your actions are perceived by others and how that can affect their attitude to you?*

- *Before you start the engine, have you taken a minute to consider your state of mind?*

- *Are you late for work, had an argument with the boss, or just out for a Sunday afternoon bimble?*

All these will affect how you ride and how you react to other road users.

BETARI'S CYCLE OF CONFLICT

Your Behaviour → My Attitude → My Behaviour → Your Attitude → Your Behaviour

- Finally, when you get off the bike at the end do you think about what went well, and what could have gone better?

- Are you learning from your riding experience?

There is however, a fourth competence that appears in the Driver Education Matrix which the Advanced Rider Course only briefly touches on in the handbook and doesn't directly assess. This concerns what we actually do when we go somewhere - the journey. Each journey is different. The commute to work is very different from a social ride at the weekend or embarking on a tour of Europe with mates. What do you need to plan for? What additional hazards may you encounter that you perhaps don't normally?

12. Beyond the Test

The Killing Zone, a book by Paul Craig, studied why private pilots died. In the book he describes how the fatality rate of pilots rose once they passed their private pilot's licence after 40 hours, and didn't lower until they had accumulated some 350-400 hours of flying. He called this the Killing Zone.

The industry investigated this at length and what they came up with was their pilot training was all about Hands and Feet flying. They spent 40 hours under the guidance of an instructor learning how to control an aeroplane and flying short distances around an airbase before landing again - the first two competences of the Driver Education matrix.

What they didn't teach was what pilots actually did once they passed their test - which was to go places. Taking the kids to the coast for the weekend. Come Sunday evening the weather's not that good but they have to get back as it's work and school tomorrow, so they push the envelope yet don't have the experience to make the right decisions both before take-off or during the flight.

As a result of these studies pilot training completely changed around 15 years ago to a concept of scenario-based flight training to build experience of journeys and to build airmanship faster than just flight hours. They also put greater emphasis on ensuring pilots understand Human Factors as the root of good risk management and decision making.

Much of motorcycle tuition and testing still centres on 'hands and feet' control and managing traffic on local roads. What few training organisations do is coach riders how to plan and manage a long distance journey. Somehow we're expected to do this for ourselves and many have come to grief by setting off on journeys beyond their experience or without adequately planning the 'what if' scenarios that often come into play on longer trips.

So think about your next big journey before you set out. If it's a long trip where the SatNav says it's 6 hours riding, think about stops. Few people can ride for 6 hours without a comfort break, fuel and food. In hot weather, dehydration can take its toll and your concentration levels will drop without you noticing. Adding in stops for fuel and refreshments could mean your journey has become possibly 8 hours long - a full day's riding for most, not just a long morning. Also, are you riding on the right-hand side of the road if in Europe? Are you having to concentrate more? What happens if one of your group breaks down? Do you have tools, breakdown cover, etc? What happens if you can't make it to the hotel tonight? Do you have a Plan B or are you just going to push on regardless?

There are organisations that run accompanied tours, both around the UK and abroad. These are no soft options for wimps. If you've not been on a longer journey, stayed away overnight, planned a riding weekend over unfamiliar and challenging roads (which is why we go there) one of these could be a good way to safely extend your envelope of experience.

With the routes already planned along with stopping places for coffee, lunch, fuel, etc., a lot of pressure is taken off the first-timer doing a longer trip. The rewards of opening up the world of motorcycle touring, with the friendships this always forges, is well worth exploring. These longer trips can also help you build your roadcraft in advance of road miles, reducing your vulnerability, and help you become a more experienced biker, ready to plan longer journeys of your own and to get much more out of your riding career.

Lunch stop at a café somewhere in France